NORTH CAROLINA

NORTH CAROLINA

HELLO

U.S.A.

by Andrea Schulz

Jefferson-Madison
Regional Library
Charlottesville, Virginia

Lerner Publications Company

You'll find this picture of the Great Smoky Mountains at the beginning of each chapter in this book. More than 200 species of trees cover these mountains, which are shared with Tennessee to the west. Large amounts of oxygen from the densely packed trees creates the humid, "smoky" atmosphere that gives this mountain range its name.

Cover (left): Nichols Ranch near Wayensville, North Carolina. Cover (right): A red train car used by the Swain County Chamber of Commerce. Pages 2–3: Chimney Rock in North Carolina. Page 3: A replica of the Wright Brothers' airplane.

This book is available in two editions:
Library binding by Lerner Publications Company, a division of Lerner Publishing Group
Soft cover by First Avenue Editions, an imprint of Lerner Publishing Group
241 First Avenue North
Minneapolis, MN 55401 U.S.A.

Website address: www.lernerbooks.com

Library of Congress Cataloging-in-Publication Data

Schulz, Andrea.
    North Carolina / by Andrea Schulz.— (Revised and expanded 2nd edition)
        p.   cm. — (Hello U.S.A.)
    Includes index.
    ISBN: 0–8225–4072–X (lib. bdg. : alk. paper)
    ISBN: 0–8225–4137–8 (pbk. : alk. paper)
    1. North Carolina—Juvenile literature. [1. North Carolina.]
    I. Title. II. Series.
F254.3.S38 2002
975.6—dc21
                                                            2001001165

Manufactured in the United States of America
1 2 3 4 5 6 – JR – 07 06 05 04 03 02

CONTENTS

North Carolina's mountainsides are covered with rhododendron blossoms in the spring.

THE LAND

Islands to Appalachians

Some North Carolinians think of their state as a place of sandy beaches, grassy islands, and dark, swampy **wetlands**. Others picture a piece of hilly farmland or a busy city as home. Still other North Carolinians look out their windows and see pine-covered mountain peaks and deep valleys. Although each view is different, each is part of North Carolina.

Located in the southeastern part of the United States, North Carolina is bordered on the north by Virginia. To the south lie South Carolina and Georgia. Tennessee is North Carolina's neighbor to the west. The Atlantic Ocean washes up against North Carolina's entire eastern edge.

Many bald cypress trees grow in North Carolina's swamplands.

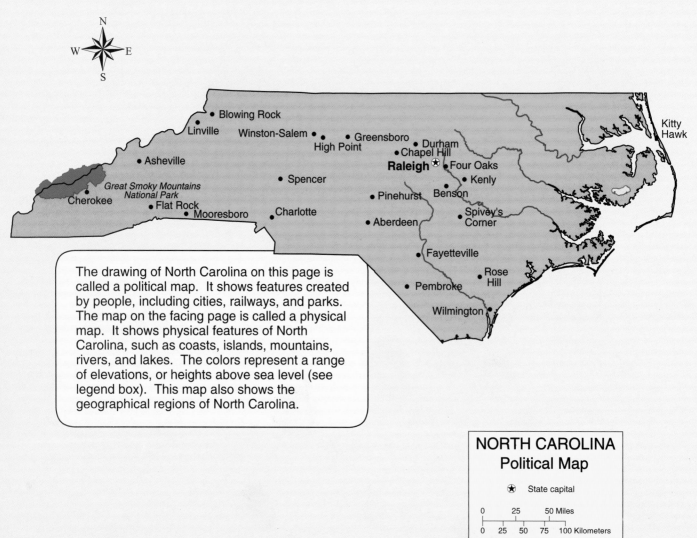

The drawing of North Carolina on this page is called a political map. It shows features created by people, including cities, railways, and parks. The map on the facing page is called a physical map. It shows physical features of North Carolina, such as coasts, islands, mountains, rivers, and lakes. The colors represent a range of elevations, or heights above sea level (see legend box). This map also shows the geographical regions of North Carolina.

Blowing Rock
Linville
Winston-Salem
Greensboro
High Point
Durham
Chapel Hill
Asheville
Raleigh ✪ Four Oaks
Spencer
Kenly
Great Smoky Mountains National Park
Benson
Cherokee
Pinehurst
Flat Rock
Spivey's Corner
Mooresboro
Charlotte
Aberdeen
Fayetteville
Rose Hill
Pembroke
Wilmington
Kitty Hawk

NORTH CAROLINA
Political Map

✪   State capital

0   25   50 Miles

0   25   50   75   100 Kilometers

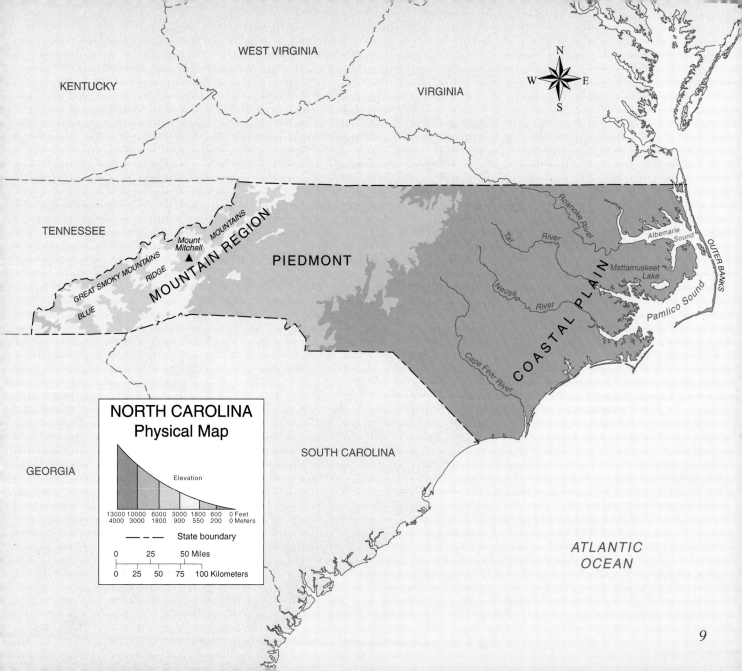

WEST VIRGINIA

KENTUCKY

VIRGINIA

N
W E
S

TENNESSEE

Mount
Mitchell ▲
GREAT SMOKY MOUNTAINS
BLUE
RIDGE
MOUNTAINS
MOUNTAIN REGION

PIEDMONT

Roanoke River
Tar
River
Albemarle
Sound
Mattamuskeet
Lake
Neuse
River
COASTAL PLAIN
OUTER BANKS
Pamlico Sound

Cape Fear River

NORTH CAROLINA
Physical Map

Elevation

| 13000 | 10000 | 6000 | 3000 | 1800 | 600 | 0 Feet |
| 4000 | 3000 | 1800 | 900 | 550 | 200 | 0 Meters |

- - - State boundary

0   25   50 Miles

0   25   50   75   100 Kilometers

GEORGIA

SOUTH CAROLINA

ATLANTIC
OCEAN

The **Outer Banks**—a long, narrow strip of sand islands just off the Atlantic coast—serve as a fragile barrier protecting North Carolina from ocean storms. Powerful ocean currents cause shifting sands, and sudden storms are common off the Outer Banks's shores. As a result, this area has witnessed many shipwrecks. The waters between the Outer Banks and the mainland are known as **sounds.** Two of the state's largest sounds are Pamlico and Albemarle.

North Carolina is divided into three regions—the

Pieces of an old ship rest in the sand at Cape Hatteras.

Coastal Plain, the Piedmont, and the Mountain Region. The flat Coastal Plain covers eastern North Carolina. Marshes (grassy wetlands) and swamps (wooded wetlands), including the Great Dismal Swamp, soak part of the eastern half of the Coastal Plain. Much of the fertile land in the western half of this region is planted with tobacco and other crops. Low hills of sand roll through the southwestern part of the Coastal Plain.

The grassy wetlands of the Coastal Plain are home to many types of water birds.

West of the Coastal Plain lies the hilly Piedmont. The two regions are separated by the **Fall Line**—an imaginary line marking the drop from the highlands of the Piedmont to the lowlands of the Coastal Plain. Rolling, wooded hills, wide fields, and most of the state's people and cities can be found in the Piedmont.

The city of Charlotte lies on the Piedmont.

The Great Smokies are often covered by layers of fog.

In the Mountain Region, the Blue Ridge and Great Smoky mountain ranges cut a jagged path across western North Carolina. These two ranges are part of the Appalachians, a chain of mountains extending from Canada to Alabama. Mount Mitchell, the highest peak in the eastern United States, rises 6,684 feet in North Carolina's Mountain Region.

Rivers race down from the Mountain Region and join other waterways in the Piedmont. Many of the rivers then flow through the Coastal Plain and into the Atlantic Ocean. Some of the state's most important rivers are the Roanoke, the Tar, the Neuse, and the Cape Fear.

A waterfall, one of many in North Carolina, cascades down a forest hill.

Most of North Carolina's lakes are artificial. They were formed when dams were built across the state's rivers to hold back water. Lake Mattamuskeet and a few other natural lakes can be found on the Coastal Plain.

North Carolina's temperatures vary along with its regions. The average summertime temperature on the Coastal Plain is 80° F, while the Mountain Region averages 70° F. The Coastal Plain has warmer winters, too. Temperatures there average 48° F compared to 28° F in the mountains.

A generous 50 inches of **precipitation** (rain, snow, sleet, and hail) is measured each year in North Carolina. Most of the snow falls in the mountains.

Many different kinds of plants and animals thrive in North Carolina. Forests cover about two-thirds of the state. Pine and cypress trees grow on the Coastal Plain. Oaks, hickories, and evergreens are common in the Piedmont and Mountain regions. Flowering trees and shrubs such as azaleas, camellias, dogwoods, and rhododendrons bloom all over the state. Venus's-flytrap, an insect-eating plant, grows wild in the pine forests of the Coastal Plain.

A dogwood tree blooms on a hillside in the Blue Ridge Mountains.

Bears, deer, foxes, wild turkeys, opossums, river otters, and beavers make their homes in forests and along rivers throughout North Carolina. Thousands of ducks and geese spend winters in the marshes and swamps of the Coastal Plain. Wild horses gallop along a few of the islands of the Outer Banks, and loggerhead turtles lay their eggs on the islands' shores. Dolphins and whales can be spotted swimming off North Carolina's coast.

Ghost crabs *(top left)* and wild horses *(bottom left)* are just two kinds of animals that call North Carolina home.

THE HISTORY

Natives and Newcomers

any thousands of years ago, the first people to enter North America crossed a land bridge that once connected the continent to Asia. As time passed, some of these Indians, or Native Americans, traveled farther and farther south and east. Along the way, they hunted large mastodons (elephantlike animals) and beavers as big as bears. The Indians probably reached the area that later became North Carolina about 11,000 years ago.

Town Creek Indian Mound, a prehistoric ceremonial site, dates back to A.D. 1200.

Scientists reconstructed this ceremonial building by studying the site of Town Creek Indian Mound in Montgomery County, North Carolina.

About 3,000 years later, many of the large animals in North America died out. The Indians started hunting smaller animals such as deer and squirrels. Later groups built villages and planted fields of corn, gourds, and squash. They also fished and gathered seeds, berries, nuts, and roots to eat. By the 1500s, several Indian nations lived in the area of North Carolina.

A large and powerful group known as the Cherokee Nation occupied much of the area. Their homeland stretched across the mountains and valleys of the southern Appalachians. Each Cherokee village had two chiefs—one who solved daily problems and one who took charge during wars. Villagers grew many crops, including corn, beans, pumpkins, and tobacco. They shot deer with bows and arrows and caught fish with spears, traps, and hooks.

In south central North Carolina, the Catawba lived in villages of as many as 100 people. The Catawba constructed their houses using bark for the walls and cattails for thatched roofs. Large fields of vegetables surrounded the villages. In both Catawba and Cherokee communities, the women farmed and the men hunted.

Many Indians lived along the Atlantic coast. One group, the Tuscarora, built their villages along the Roanoke, Pamlico, and Neuse Rivers. The Pamlico Indians lived to the south of the Tuscarora.

The Cherokee made what were called booger masks from hornets' nests. Soldiers wore the masks during booger dances to make fun of their enemies before battles.

Various groups of coastal Indians all followed similar ways of life. They hollowed out tree trunks that were 50 feet long to make canoes for traveling and fishing. To catch fish, the men dragged nets through the water or pierced the fish with sharp spears. The women tended fields that were sometimes as large as 200 acres. Using frames made from wooden poles, coastal Indians built rectangular houses covered with bark or woven mats.

Indian women molded clay pots for cooking food. They also treated animal hides to make leather, which was cut and sewn into clothing.

Indians who lived near the Atlantic Coast often caught fish and smoked them over a large bonfire.

Coastal Indians probably greeted the area's first European visitor—Giovanni da Verrazano. An explorer hired by France, Verrazano sailed into the location that became Cape Fear in 1524. Sixteen years later, Spanish explorer Hernando de Soto traveled through the area's southwestern mountains. As he traveled, de Soto captured, tortured, and killed many American Indians.

In the 1580s, British explorers twice tried to build **colonies,** or settlements, in the region of North Carolina. But both colonies failed. The first successful British colony was built in 1607 in the area that later became Virginia.

Giovanni da Verrazano was the first European to explore the Atlantic Coast.

The Lost Colony

A group of British colonists landed on Roanoke Island in 1587. Led by John White, their governor, the settlers quickly built homes. With the help of Indians who lived nearby, the colonists gathered food in the forest. A month later, White's daughter gave birth to the first British baby born in North America—Virginia Dare.

Governor White soon had to sail back to Great Britain for supplies. When he arrived, he learned that a war with Spain had begun. All British ships were needed to fight the Spanish. White could not return to his colony until three years later.

When he finally reached Roanoke Island, Governor White found it deserted. All the colonists had disappeared. The only clue was the name of an island, "Croatoan," carved into a tree. But before White could search Croatoan Island for the colonists, a storm hit and forced him to sail out to sea.

Later searches failed to find clues to the mystery of the Lost Colony. However, some people think that the colonists joined one of the Indian tribes living near Croatoan Island (later called Hatteras Island). Many of the Lumbee Indians, who live in southeastern North Carolina, have British names. Some Lumbees have blue eyes and light hair, features that may come from white ancestors. Perhaps the Lumbees' ancestors were the settlers of the Lost Colony.

This engraving shows the English colonists first arriving at Roanoke Island.

As more colonists settled in North America, Great Britain strengthened its claim on the continent. In 1663 Charles II, the British king, gave a piece of land to some wealthy friends. Called *Carolina* (the Latin name for "Charles"), the territory stretched south from the British colony of Virginia to the Spanish colony of Florida.

Soon shiploads of British people arrived in the colony of Carolina. Most of these settlers built their homes and farms near Albemarle Sound. They were soon joined by other colonists from Virginia

Ships carrying barrels of food and other goods arrived at Carolina's docks from Europe.

and Pennsylvania, and by more new **immigrants** from countries such as Great Britain, Germany, Switzerland, and France.

Most of the Indians in the colony were friendly to the settlers. Indians taught settlers how to gather and plant food, and helped them fight unfriendly nations. But in return, many of the settlers were not as generous. Instead, they took land from the Indians. Merchants cheated the Indians in trading. Slave traders came and kidnapped some Indians to sell as slaves in the West Indies—a group of islands south of Florida.

In 1710 a group of settlers built the village of New Bern near the Neuse River, on a piece of land stolen from the Tuscarora Indians. The Indians rebelled. Tuscarora soldiers, who were later joined by other groups of Indians, attacked white settlements near the river.

For both Indians and colonists, corn was an important food crop.

The Tuscarora War began when Tuscarora Indians captured two colonists and an African slave. This picture, drawn by one of the prisoners, shows the trial at which the colonists were accused of stealing Tuscarora land.

Known as the Tuscarora War, the series of battles continued for two years until the colonists defeated the Tuscarora. Most of the Tuscarora who survived the war eventually moved north to the colony of New York.

In 1712 Carolina was divided into three separate colonies—North Carolina, South Carolina, and Georgia. North Carolina became one of 13 British colonies on the Atlantic coast. Settlers continued to arrive in North Carolina from the other colonies, and more immigrants came from Scotland, Germany, and several other northern European countries. By the 1760s, 130,000 people were living in North Carolina.

Because they were under the rule of faraway Great Britain, North Carolina and the other 12 colonies had to follow British laws. But the colonies wanted to govern themselves. The colonists also felt it was unfair to be taxed by Great Britain. The North American colonies began planning to break away from Great Britain so they could form their own country.

The war between Great Britain and the colonies, known as the American Revolution, broke out in 1775. On July 4, 1776, representatives from all of the 13 colonies signed the Declaration of Independence, claiming freedom from British rule.

The British governor of North Carolina, William Tryon, tried to keep angry colonists from fighting against the British government in 1765.

The colonies won the American Revolution seven years later and began to organize a new nation. North Carolina joined the United States as the 12th state on November 21, 1789.

Farmers hauled their hay, cotton, tobacco, and other crops to market on roads made out of wooden planks. North Carolinians later abandoned many of these roads when they realized how difficult they were to repair.

Throughout the early 1800s, most people in central and western North Carolina worked on small farms, growing just enough food to feed their families and their livestock. Some settlers in eastern North Carolina owned **plantations,** large farms where black slaves planted and worked fields of tobacco and cotton. A smaller number of African Americans were free and had jobs as carpenters, mechanics, barbers, and tailors. Black people made up about one-third of the state's population by 1860.

Keeping Tradition Alive

During the mid-1800s, most of the Indians of the Cherokee Nation were removed from their traditional land in the Appalachians. They were forced to go west to a reservation, or land set aside by the U.S. government for Native Americans. But about 1,000 Cherokee refused to leave their homeland. After many years of fighting for their rights, the Eastern Band of Cherokee in North Carolina was eventually allowed to govern itself. By remaining in their homeland, the Cherokee could continue to pass on their traditions and ways of life to their children and grandchildren.

Ayunini, or Swimmer, was a Cherokee leader and medicine man. He helped preserve his culture by writing down ancient Cherokee traditions.

Workers scraped pine trees for resin, a gummy substance used to make turpentine.

   North Carolinians near the coast made turpentine
and tar from tree sap, and carved tree trunks into
masts. All three items were used to build ships.
Fishers made a living by netting shad and herring
from the state's rivers and shellfish from the coastal
waters.

Gold mining became big business in North Carolina during the 1800s. The first gold discovered in the United States was found in the state.

While Southern states such as North Carolina depended mostly on farming for money, Northerners made much of their money from manufacturing. While many Southern plantations used slaves, slavery was illegal in Northern states. Many people wanted to make it illegal in the South as well. But Southerners argued that they needed free slave labor to earn a living.

Early in 1861, six Southern states broke away from the Union, or United States, to form a separate country—the Confederate States of America. In North Carolina, one out of four families owned slaves. Many North Carolinians did not want to join the Confederacy. But when President Abraham Lincoln sent Northern troops to keep the South in the Union, North Carolina was forced to take sides. North Carolinians did not want to fight against their neighbors to the south, so they joined the Confederacy at the outbreak of the Civil War.

The Tar Heel State

North Carolina has been known as the Tar Heel State for a long time, but no one is really sure where the nickname came from. Tar, however, was an important part of North Carolina's economy in the 1800s.

The most common story told by Tarheels credits the state's Confederate soldiers with earning the nickname. During a difficult Civil War battle, North Carolina's soldiers were fighting side by side with troops from a neighboring state. When the going got tough, legend says that the other Confederates ran away, leaving North Carolina's soldiers to battle the enemy alone.

When the two groups later met up, the troops who had fled teased the North Carolinians about being from a state full of tar makers. The Tarheels replied that the soldiers who fled needed some tar on their own heels to "stick" better to the next battle!

By the time the North won the war in 1865, one-fourth of all the Confederate soldiers who had been killed were from North Carolina. Many of the survivors found that their homes, farms, and crops had been destroyed. Slaves were freed, but many of them had no money, no job, and no place to live.

U.S. troops moved into North Carolina to oversee **Reconstruction,** or the rebuilding of the South. To rejoin the United States, each former Confederate state had to pass a law giving African American men the right to vote. North Carolina was readmitted to the Union in 1868.

African Americans meet to talk about an upcoming election.

The state slowly recovered from the war. Many farmers returned to planting their fields. Other people began to build cotton mills and factories for processing tobacco and making furniture. By the late 1800s, thousands of North Carolinians were busy making fabrics, cigarettes, and tables and chairs from the state's supply of cotton, tobacco, and lumber.

But the new jobs did not benefit all Tarheels. Many of the factories would not hire African Americans. Life was difficult for black North Carolinians in other ways, too. In the 1890s, state politicians passed **Jim Crow laws.** These laws prevented black people from going to the same schools as white people. They also separated blacks and whites in bus stations, movie theaters, restrooms, and other public places. At the same time, lawmakers in North Carolina kept most African Americans from voting. Without voting rights, blacks had no way to change the laws.

At a fabric mill, a young worker learns to examine spools of thread.

Members of the Ku Klux Klan wore costumes to hide their identities. They threatened, beat, and killed many African Americans and their white friends.

In the early 1900s, North Carolinians worked to improve education in the state, opening nearly 160 new high schools in rural areas and establishing public libraries in many towns. The state also built new and better roads and highways, earning North Carolina another nickname—the Good Roads State.

North Carolina's factories grew during World War I (1914–1918) and World War II (1939–1945). Workers manufactured tons of ammunition, millions of cigarettes, and miles of fabric for uniforms to send to the soldiers fighting in Europe. The factories didn't stop after the wars, either. By 1950 North Carolinians were leading the nation in the production of towels, socks, underwear, and tobacco products.

The 1950s also marked the start of the **civil rights movement.** African Americans in North Carolina and throughout the nation banded together to fight for equal rights. The U.S. government ruled in 1954 that black students and white students must be allowed to attend the same schools. By 1960 black students in the Tar Heel State were attending what had once been all-white schools.

Dorothy Counts *(center)* is taunted by white students as she enters Harding High School in Charlotte. She is one of the first black students to attend this school.

That same year, four black college students sat down in a whites-only restaurant in Greensboro, North Carolina, and refused to leave until they were served. Their peaceful protest grew as more and more people joined them every day. It finally paid off when city officials agreed to open public places to both blacks and whites. Civil rights leaders all over the South began using this same method, known as a sit-in, to force public places to serve black people.

By 1970 much progress had been made in North Carolina. The state's schools were teaching black students and white students in the same class-rooms, and most public places were open to people of both races. Laws were passed to make sure that men and women of all races had the right to vote.

Greensboro Lunch Counter Sit-ins

On February 1, 1960, four college students sat down and asked for coffee at a Woolworth lunch counter in Greensboro. No one would serve them, but they stayed until the lunch counter closed that evening. The students went back the next day and waited again to be served. More African Americans soon occupied 63 of the 65 seats at the counter.

By the end of the week, more than 300 students—both blacks and whites—were participating in sit-ins at various restaurants and lunch counters throughout the city. Sit-ins soon spread to other cities in North Carolina.

On July 25, 1960, the first African American was finally served at the Woolworth lunch counter in Greensboro where the sit-ins began.

Four Greensboro college students protest segregation by holding a sit-in at a Woolworth lunch counter.

The Tar Heel State saw some big economic changes in the 1980s. Textile factories were hurt because cloth from other countries became cheaper. Some of the state's textile mills closed. The nation's demand for cigarettes dropped, as Americans learned that smoking is dangerous to their health. Tobacco growers and processors began selling much of their tobacco to other countries.

In 1999 the East Coast was hit by Hurricane Floyd. Seventy percent of eastern North Carolina was submerged in water. About 2.6 million people, including many North Carolinians, had to be evacuated from their homes along the Atlantic Ocean.

Even with these challenges, the state's economy has remained strong. North Carolinians are working to attract new businesses and create new jobs. Research Triangle Park near Raleigh, for example, has become the workplace of thousands of scientists and researchers. North Carolinians still manufacture textiles, tobacco, and furniture. They also make chemicals, computers, and telephone equipment, and have many other types of jobs as well.

PEOPLE & ECONOMY

Tarheels at Work and Play

More than 8 million people live in North Carolina. About half of these residents live in the country or in small towns, but more and more people are moving to the state's urban centers, or cities. Some people come to study at the state's universities or to find work with new high-tech companies. Other Tarheels try starting their own businesses.

North Carolina's largest cities—Charlotte, Greensboro, Raleigh (the state capital), Winston-Salem, and Durham—are in the Piedmont region. Wilmington, located on the Atlantic coast, is North Carolina's largest port city.

About 70 percent of all North Carolinians have ancestors from Great Britian, Scotland, Germany,

and other European countries. African Americans
make up 21 percent of the state's population.
North Carolina's Latino population grew from
1 percent in 1990 to almost 5 percent in 2000.
Asian Americans make up about 1 percent of
North Carolina's population.

Half of North
Carolina's population
lives in rural areas.
Many young people
who live in the
country care for
horses and other
animals.

A Cherokee boatbuilder makes a dugout canoe in the traditional way.

About 10,000 Cherokee Indians live on Qualla Boundary, a reservation in the western corner of the state. The Lumbees—believed by some people to have ancestors from North Carolina's Lost Colony— live in and around the city of Pembroke. Many Native Americans study at Pembroke State University, one of only a few colleges in the eastern United States to offer a degree in American Indian studies.

At the Reed Gold Mine State Historic Site, young visitors pan for gold.

Tarheels preserve their past at a variety of historical landmarks. For example, the Wright Brothers National Memorial stands near Kitty Hawk on the Outer Banks. Here, Orville and Wilbur Wright made the first motor-powered airplane flight in the world in 1903.

In Kenly, the Tobacco Museum of North Carolina traces the history of tobacco farming and processing in the state. History buffs can experience a bit of old-fashioned farm life at the Malcolm Blue Historical Farm in Aberdeen. And at the North Carolina Transportation Museum in Spencer, visitors can ride trains that have been carrying passengers for over 100 years.

North Carolinians also celebrate many festivals. Bluegrass musicians play their fiddles and banjos at the Snuffy Jenkins Old Time and Bluegrass Music Festival in Mooresboro and at other bluegrass events around the state. Gospel singers from all over the country come to North Carolina to perform every year during their meeting in Benson. The National Hollerin' Contest, in Spivey's Corner, recalls the days when farmers talked across their fields by shouting.

A carnival performer strolls around on stilts at one of North Carolina's many summer festivals.

North Carolinians enjoy all kinds of water fun, from rafting *(left)* to speeding down Sliding Rock *(below)*—a natural, slippery water slide.

Fishers, boaters, and swimmers enjoy North Carolina's rivers, lakes, and ocean shores. The state's mountain peaks attract hikers and downhill skiers. Adventure seekers can explore mountain caves, such as Linville Caverns. Golfers flock to North Carolina's hundreds of golf courses. In fact, they like the state so much that the Professional Golfers Association located its World Golf Hall of Fame in Pinehurst.

Hikers can rent tame llamas to carry packs on long trips through the rugged wilderness of the Blue Ridge Mountains.

Sports fans in the Tar Heel State cheer for North Carolina's professional teams including the Charlotte Hornets in basketball; the Carolina Hurricanes hockey team; and the Carolina Panthers on the football field. College teams, like the Blue Devils of Duke University in Durham, also draw large crowds.

In addition to recreation, North Carolina offers its residents a wide variety of jobs to choose from. Almost half of all working North Carolinians provide services to other people or businesses.

Some of the state's service workers are bank tellers, doctors, or clerks in stores. Many people have service jobs in the offices and laboratories of Research Triangle Park near Raleigh. Researchers there explore new ideas and products in areas including medicine, chemistry, education, electronics, and forestry.

Service workers in North Carolina include truck drivers. Police officers work for the government.

A technician examines a computer part.

Fifteen percent of North Carolinians work for the government. These workers operate the state's public schools, military bases, and courts of law. Soldiers at Camp Lejeune Marine Corps Base on the coast are trained to work on navy ships. Fort Bragg is where the U.S. Army's special forces are trained.

About one out of every five jobholders in North Carolina works in manufacturing—more than in any other state. The Tar Heel State continues to lead all other states in the manufacturing of tobacco products, textiles, and wooden furniture. Greensboro has three of the world's largest textile factories. High Point's textile workers make nearly one million pairs of socks and nylon stockings every day. High Point is also known for its many furniture factories.

Medicines and other chemicals are manufactured in North Carolina. Some workers in the Tar Heel State assemble high-tech electronic equipment, such as computers and telephones. North Carolinians also package many food products, including meats, beverages, and baked goods.

Tobacco companies buy much of their tobacco from farmers in North Carolina. In fact, the state's farmers grow more tobacco than any other crop. North Carolina's fields of corn, soybeans, peanuts, sweet potatoes, and strawberries are also important money-makers. Two-thirds of the state's apples come from Henderson County, which is in the Mountain Region. Almost a million apple trees grow in that county alone. Farmers in North Carolina also raise chickens, hogs, and more turkeys than any other state.

On a tobacco farm, a young North Carolinian helps out during harvesttime.

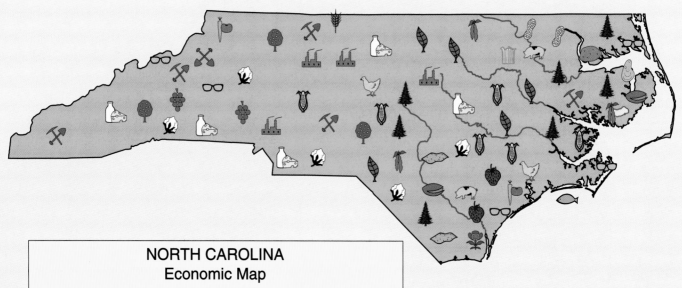

NORTH CAROLINA
Economic Map

The symbols on this map show where different economic activities take place in North Carolina. The legend below explains what each symbol stands for.

				Soybeans
Berries	Forest products	Nursery products	Stone	
Clay	Fruit	Oysters	Sweet potatoes	
Corn	Grapes	Peanuts	Tobacco	
Cotton	Hay	Pecans	Tourism	
Dairy products	Hogs	Potatoes	Vegetables	
Fish	Manufacturing	Poultry	Wheat	

A fisher checks the large, cagelike trap he uses to catch shellfish.

North Carolina fishers haul in about $100 million worth of fish, crabs, clams, and shrimp every year from the state's rivers and coastal waters. Workers at fish hatcheries raise catfish, crayfish, and trout in artificial ponds. They then catch and sell the adult fish.

THE ENVIRONMENT

Keeping the Waters Clean

For thousands of years, North Carolina's rivers and streams have been home to many kinds of plants and fish. Animals and people living near the waterways have enjoyed fresh, clear water and have caught plenty of healthy fish to eat.

But over the last 10 years or so, things have changed. Of the state's more than 38,000 miles of streams and rivers, about 2,400 miles, or 6 percent, have become seriously polluted. Pollution threatens the plants and animals that are dependent on these waters for survival.

North Carolina's Broad River is lined with towns and farmland.

Two common pollutants in North Carolina's waterways are the chemical **nutrients** nitrogen and phosphorus. In small amounts, these nutrients help plants and animals grow. But too much of the nutrients can harm living creatures in the state's waterways.

Nitrogen and phosphorus are used to make many products, such as cleaners, dyes, and medicines. But when these chemicals are emptied down drains, they end up in household wastewater. Factories and businesses that produce or use the chemicals also discharge them into their wastewater.

Most of North Carolina's wastewater travels through pipes to sewage treatment plants. There, the water is treated to filter out chemicals, solids, and harmful bacteria and is then emptied into rivers. But many sewage treatment plants are not equipped to remove the nitrogen and phosphorus, which are then released into rivers.

Nitrogen and phosphorus also enter rivers from farmland. As ingredients in fertilizers, the nutrients are applied to crops each year to help them grow.

Rainwater carries away any extra fertilizer in its path when it runs off the fields.

But when farmers use too much fertilizer, rain washes the excess nitrogen and phosphorus into rivers. People in cities and towns add to the problem when they put fertilizer on their lawns and gardens. Rain then carries any extra fertilizer into storm sewers, which empty into rivers.

This waterway is smothered by a thick layer of algae.

When rivers are overloaded with nitrogen and phosphorus, rootless plants called algae feed on the nutrients and spread quickly over the surface of the water. Thick mats of algae keep sunlight from reaching deeper water, where plants that produce oxygen need the light to survive.

Without light, these deepwater plants die. The loss of the oxygen they produce is deadly to fish and other water animals that need oxygen to survive. The amount of oxygen in the water decreases further when the thick mats of algae die. As the algae decay, they use up even more oxygen.

Run-off from farmland turns clear waterways a muddy brown.

The nutrients that enter rivers from farmland and from gardens are carried by sediment (soil particles that can slide into the water). Sediment is the number-one source of pollution in North Carolina's rivers, making the water muddy, clogging the waterways, and affecting animal habitats. During rainstorms, soil that is washed down sloping fields and yards eventually enters streams and rivers.

Sediment also enters waterways when shopping centers, houses, and roads are built. During construction, heavy machinery is used to dig up soil. If special fences are not used, sediment can slide away from the site and clog waterways. Sediment also comes from dirt roads used to carry logs out of the forest for the lumber industry.

Sediment can fill in shallow rivers, stopping the flow of water and blocking the path of water creatures. And by making water muddy, sediment—like algae—prevents sunlight from reaching underwater plants. As the sediment settles, it coats the riverbed, smothering the plants and animals that live there.

North Carolinians are working to stop the damage to their waters. The state has passed laws to limit the amount of phosphorus and nitrogen that factories and sewage treatment plants can empty into rivers. Other laws protect wetlands and plants that grow along waterways. These natural barriers help prevent the nutrients in farm and urban run-off from reaching the rivers. Researchers also are developing ways to reduce the amount of nutrients in wastewater.

Dirty water *(above, top)* can make it harder for fish such as brook trout *(above)* to breathe.

The state has begun working with farmers and landowners to prevent nutrients and sediment from running off North Carolina's fields, yards, and gardens. And state laws say that construction projects cannot begin without an approved plan to control the loss of sediment.

North Carolinians can help protect a waterway in their state by joining the Stream Watch program. Stream watchers learn how to spot nutrients, sediment, and other forms of pollution. Stream Watch groups also hold nature walks to teach other concerned citizens about water pollution.

Some of North Carolina's farms have begun collecting their wastewater in large holding ponds, where sediment and fertilizer can sink to the bottom. The water is then drained and allowed to enter waterways.

By testing water regularly, scientists can tell when a river needs help.

When stream watchers see signs of pollution in their river, they can notify North Carolina's Department of Environment and Natural Resources. The state then tries to find the source of the pollution and begins to work on improving the river's water quality.

With new state programs aimed at fighting water pollution, North Carolinians can save their rivers from more serious damage. By working together, the state's residents hope to make their waterways clean again.

Fun Facts

Blackbeard, a widely feared pirate, was beheaded in 1718 at Ocracoke Inlet off North Carolina's coast. Legend says that Blackbeard's ghost still roams the coast in search of his head.

The lighthouse at Cape Hatteras, North Carolina, is the tallest in the United States.

Cape Hatteras is nicknamed "Graveyard of the Atlantic" because many shipwrecks occurred in its waters. Shifting sands are thought to be the cause.

More denim is made in Greensboro, North Carolina, than in any other place in the world.

After Blackbeard was beheaded, his head was hung from a pole on a ship.

Kill Devil Hill near Kitty Hawk, North Carolina, was the site of the world's first motor-powered airplane flight. In 1903 Orville and Wilbur Wright flew their plane a distance of 120 feet.

Grandfather Mountain in North Carolina has the highest swinging bridge in the United States. It hangs 1 mile above the ground.

Fayetteville, North Carolina, is home to the oldest miniature golf course in the United States.

The world's largest frying pan is said to be in Rose Hill, North Carolina. The pan, which measures 15 feet across, is used to fry more than 250 whole chickens at a time during the town's festivals.

Inventors Orville and Wilbur Wright test an early airplane. Orville acts as test pilot, and Wilbur observes the takeoff.

STATE SONG

The state song of North Carolina was written by William Gaston
and arranged by Mrs. E. E. Randolph. It was adopted as
the official state song by the General Assembly of 1927.

THE OLD NORTH STATE

Words by William Gaston and music by E.E. Randolph

You can hear "The Old North State" by visiting this website:
<http://www.50states.com/songs/ncarolin.htm>

A NORTH CAROLINA RECIPE

North Carolina grows more sweet potatoes each year than any other state. In 1995 North Carolinians adopted this bright orange treat as their state vegetable. With the recipe below, you can have sweet potatoes for breakfast!

SWEET POTATO WAFFLES

¼ cup butter
1½ cup flour
3 teaspoons baking powder
1 teaspoon salt

¼ teaspoon nutmeg
3 eggs, separated
1 cup milk
1 cup sweet potatoes, cooked and mashed

1. To prepare sweet potato (large one should be enough), first prick four holes in its skin with fork, then microwave it for about 10 minutes. If you don't have a microwave, boil it for about 20 minutes.
2. Ask an adult to help you remove the skin. Then mash sweet potato with a fork.
3. Melt butter and set aside.
4. In large bowl, mix together flour, baking powder, salt, and nutmeg.
5. Separate eggs.
6. In another bowl, beat egg yolk and combine with milk, sweet potato, and melted butter.
7. Stir this mixture into dry ingredients.
8. With electric mixer, beat egg yolks until they are fluffy and white, then stir very gently into sweet potato batter.
9. Now batter is ready for the waffle iron. Follow manufacturer's directions when using the waffle iron.

Makes 4 waffles.

HISTORICAL TIMELINE

9000 B.C. Indians move into the area that later became North Carolina.

A.D. 1524 Giovanni da Verrazano explores Cape Fear.

1587 Virginia Dare is the first British baby born in North America. She is born August 18, 1587, on Roanoke Island.

1590 John White returns to Roanoke Island and finds it deserted.

1710 The village of New Bern is built near the Neuse River.

1712 The Tuscarora War begins and lasts for two years. Carolina is divided into three separate colonies—North Carolina, South Carolina, and Georgia.

1718 Blackbeard is killed near Ocracoke Island.

1776 North Carolina is one of 13 colonies to sign the Declaration of Independence, claiming freedom from British rule.

1789 North Carolina becomes the 12th state.

1792 Raleigh is named the state capital.

1795 The University of North Carolina, the nation's first state university, opens.

1838 Most Indians are forcibly removed from their lands in North Carolina and surrounding states.

1861 The Civil War begins. North Carolina secedes from the Union and joins the Confederacy.

1868 North Carolina is readmitted to the Union.

1903 The Wright Brothers fly the first motor-powered airplane near Kitty Hawk.

1950 North Carolinians lead the nation in the production of towels, socks, underwear, and tobacco products.

1959 Research Triangle Park opens near Durham.

1960 The nation's first lunch counter sit-ins are held by African American students in Greensboro.

1971 North Carolina adopts a new state constitution.

1995 The Carolina Panthers have their first football season.

1999 Hurricane Floyd hits North Carolina, causing about $1.2 billion in damages.

OUTSTANDING NORTH CAROLINIANS

Caleb Bradham

Caleb Bradham (1866–1934), a pharmacist from New Bern, North Carolina, created the first Pepsi-Cola as a treatment for dyspepsia, or indigestion. In 1902 Bradham began bottling the soft drink in the back of his drugstore.

Betsy Byars (born 1928), from Charlotte, is the author of many books for children. In 1971 Byars won a Newbery Medal for *Summer of the Swans.*

Charlotte Hawkins Brown

Charlotte Hawkins Brown (1883–1961) was an educator born in Henderson, North Carolina. Brown turned a run-down school for blacks in Sedalia, North Carolina, into a highly successful school that attracted the best African American students from across the country. Now called the Palmer Memorial Institute, the school is known for the success of its graduates.

John Coltrane

John Coltrane (1926–1967) was one of the most popular jazz musicians in the 1960s. Raised in Hamlet, North Carolina, Coltrane played the saxophone and is best remembered for songs such as "My Favorite Things" and "Chasin' the Trane."

Howard Cosell (1920–1995) began his career as a lawyer and ended up a famous sports journalist who spent 14 years on ABC's *Monday Night Football.* Cosell, who was originally from Winston-Salem, retired from broadcasting in 1992.

Howard Cosell

Elizabeth Hanford Dole (born 1936), from Salisbury, served on many presidential cabinets and as president of the American Red Cross from 1990 to 1999. She campaigned for her husband, Bob, in 1996, and ran for president herself in 2000.

Roberta Flack (born 1940) grew up in Black Mountain, North Carolina. She is a musician whose hit songs include "The First Time Ever I Saw Your Face" and "Killing Me Softly With His Song."

Roberta Flack

Ava Gardner (1922–1990), from Smithfield, North Carolina, became a Hollywood star and acted in more than 20 films by the age of 28. Her most famous movies include *Showboat*, *Night of the Iguana*, and *East Side, West Side*.

Ava Gardner

Billy Graham (born 1918) began his life in Charlotte as William Franklin Jr. As a Protestant Evangelist, Graham's accomplishments include the Billy Graham Evangelistic Association, a radio show called *Hour of Decision*, the newspaper column "My Answer," and five books.

Andy Griffith (born 1926) is an actor from Mount Airy, North Carolina. Griffith has acted in more than 30 television shows and movies. He became well known for his starring role in the *Andy Griffith Show*.

Andy Griffith

Pleasant Hanes (1845–1925), of Winston-Salem, North Carolina, launched the P. H. Hanes Knitting Company—later renamed the Hanes Corporation—in 1902, making underwear for men and boys.

Andrew Johnson (1808–1875), the 17th president of the United States, was born in Raleigh, North Carolina. After serving as vice president under Abraham Lincoln, Johnson became president when Lincoln was assassinated. Johnson was the first president to be impeached, or charged with misconduct while in office.

Pleasant Hanes

Elizabeth Koontz

Elizabeth Koontz (born 1919), from Salisbury, North Carolina, taught special education classes for students who needed extra help. In 1968 Koontz became the first African American president of the National Education Association, the nation's largest teachers' organization.

Charles Kuralt (1934–1997) was an award-winning broadcast journalist from Wilmington, North Carolina. Kuralt began his career as a newspaper reporter and then worked as a news correspondent for CBS. He eventually became an anchor for CBS News.

Meadowlark Lemon

Herman Lay (1909–1982) grew up in Charlotte and began selling potato chips out of the trunk of his car when he was 23. Six years later, he bought the company that supplied the chips and renamed it H. W. Lay & Company. Lay eventually merged his business with the Frito Company to become Frito-Lay, Inc.

Meadowlark Lemon (born 1932), from Wilmington, is also known as the Clown Prince of Basketball. Lemon was the star attraction for the Harlem Globetrotters from 1954 to 1978.

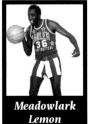

Buck Leonard

Buck Leonard (born 1907), a talented baseball player from Rocky Mount, North Carolina, was the first baseman for the Homestead Grays, a team in the National Negro League. As a black player, he was barred from the major leagues, which did not admit African Americans until 1947. Leonard was elected to the National Baseball Hall of Fame in 1972.

Floyd McKissick

Floyd McKissick (1922–1991) was a respected lawyer, civil rights leader, and minister from Asheville, North Carolina. McKissick served as the national director of the Congress of Racial Equality (CORE).

Ronnie Milsap (born 1944), from Robinsville, North Carolina, is a country musician and composer. Milsap, who has been blind since birth, is best known for hit songs such as "Any Day Now," recorded in 1982.

Ronnie Milsap

Richard Petty (born 1938) has won more races than any other stock-car racer in history. Petty won both the Daytona 500 and the NASCAR Winston Cup championships seven times. A museum honoring the racer is located near his boyhood home in Level Cross, North Carolina.

Richard Petty

James Polk (1795–1849), born in Mecklenburg County, North Carolina, became the 11th president of the United States in 1844. During Polk's presidency, the nation gained about 1 million square miles of new territory, including what became Texas, New Mexico, California, Arizona, and Oregon.

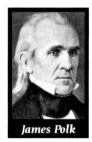

James Polk

William Sydney Porter (1862–1910), best known as O. Henry, has been called the most popular short story writer in the country. Many of his stories are funny or have a surprise ending. Two of his most famous short stories are "The Gift of the Magi" and "The Last Leaf." Porter was born in Greensboro.

Hiram Revels (1822–1901) was the first black person elected to the U.S. Senate. Born in Fayetteville, North Carolina, Revels also opened churches and schools for African Americans throughout much of the country.

Hiram Revels

Milton Supman (born 1926), known as Soupy Sales, is from Franklin, North Carolina. The comedian is best known for the *Soupy Sales Show*, which was on television in the 1960s. As part of his act, Sales has had a total of 19,000 pies thrown at him.

FACTS-AT-A-GLANCE

Nickname: Tar Heel State

Song: "The Old North State"

Motto: *Esse Quam Videri* (To Be Rather Than to Seem)

Flower: flowering dogwood

Tree: longleaf pine

Bird: cardinal

Animal: gray squirrel

Insect: honey bee

Fish: channel bass

Vegtable: sweet potato

Date and ranking of statehood: November 21, 1789, the 12th state

Capital: Raleigh

Area: 48,718 square miles

Rank in area, nationwide: 29th

Average January temperature: 41° F

Average July temperature: 70° F

North Carolina's flag's red, white, and blue colors were taken from the stars and stripes of the U.S. flag. The flag also features two dates on which documents important to the state's history were signed during the American Revolution.

POPULATION GROWTH

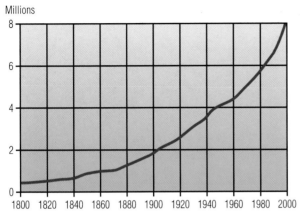

Millions

This chart shows how North Carolina's population has grown from 1800 to 2000.

North Carolina's state seal was adopted in 1984. The figures on the seal stand for important ideas for the state. The woman who is standing up represents Liberty and the woman who is sitting represents Plenty.

Population: 8,049,313 (2000 census)

Rank in population, nationwide: 11th

Major cities and populations: (2000 census) Charlotte (540,828), Raleigh (276,093), Greensboro (223,891), Durham (187,035), Winston-Salem (185,776)

U.S. senators: 2

U.S. representatives: 13

Electoral votes: 15

Natural resources: clay, feldspar, gneiss, kaolin, lumber, mica, soil, water

Agricultural products: apples, chickens, corn, dairy products, eggs, hogs, peanuts, tobacco, turkeys, soybeans, sweet potatoes

Fishing industry: Atlantic menhaden, blue crabs, catfish, clams, crayfish, flounder, shrimp, trout

Manufactured goods: chemicals, electrical equipment, food products, furniture, machinery, textiles, tobacco products

WHERE NORTH CAROLINIANS WORK

Services—56 percent (services includes jobs in trade; community, social, and personal services; finance, insurance, and real estate; transportation, communication, and utilities)

Manufacturing—19 percent

Government—15 percent

Construction—7 percent

Agriculture—3 percent

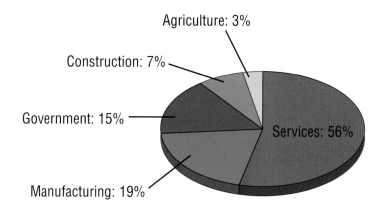

GROSS STATE PRODUCT

Services—54 percent

Manufacturing—26 percent

Government—13 percent

Construction—4 percent

Agriculture—3 percent

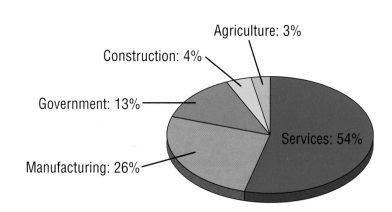

STATE WILDLIFE

Mammals: black bear, beaver, fox, gray squirrel, opossum, otter, raccoon, rabbit

Birds: cardinal, Carolina wren, duck, goose, mockingbird, mourning dove, partridge, swan

Amphibians and reptiles: American alligator, cottonmouth snake, eastern box turtle, eastern newt, river cooter, southern cricket frog, spotted salamander

Fish: bluegill, dolphin, marlin, sailfish, sturgeon, sunfish, trout

Trees: cedar, cypress, gum, hickory, oak, tulip, tupelo

Wild plants: azalea, camellia, orchid, pitcher plant, sundew, Venus's-flytrap

A pair of black bears sits on a grassy hill in the Blue Ridge Mountains.

PLACES TO VISIT

Afro-American Cultural Center, Charlotte

This arts center features art galleries and a theater dedicated to African American culture. It is housed in a historic church.

Biltmore Estate, near Asheville

The grounds surrounding this historic house cover about 8,000 acres of forest and farmland. The 250-room Biltmore Estate was completed for George Vanderbilt and his family in 1895. Visitors can view the priceless collection of furnishings and art works still on display in the house.

Bentonville Battlefield, Four Oaks

One of the most important battles of the Civil War took place at this site. There, General William T. Sherman's Union forces defeated the Confederate troops of General Joseph E. Johnston in 1865.

Carl Sandburg Home National Historic Site, Flat Rock

This national park preserves the 245-acre farm where the poet and children's author lived in his later years. Highlights include walking trails and the barn, where visitors can play with Mrs. Sandburg's goat herd.

Chimney Rock Park, near Asheville

This granite monolith rises to a height of 360 feet and can be reached by a stairway, trail, or an elevator. Parts of the movie *The Last of the Mohicans* were filmed here.

Croatan National Forest

This coastal forest covers 157,724 acres and is full of waterways and estuaries. It is the alligator's northernmost habitat in the United States and is home to a variety of insect-eating plants, including the Venus's-flytrap.

Grandfather Mountain, near Linville

This mountain is named for its resemblance to the sleeping face of an old man. Tourists can walk across a swinging bridge more than one mile above the gorge.

Morehead Planetarium, Chapel Hill

The original Apollo astronauts and many since have trained in this planetarium, one of the largest in the country. Tourists can learn all about the constellations and take in a laser light show.

Oconaluftee Indian Village, Cherokee

This village is a replica of a Cherokee community from the 1700s. Cherokee guides explain the history, culture, and life style of their ancestors. Near to the village is mile-long nature trail.

Ocracoke Island

Located about 30 miles off of North Carolina's shore, this island was once a hideout of Blackbeard. It was the site of many ship-wrecks, some of which can be seen from a boat tour.

Tweetsie Railroad, near Blowing Rock

At North Carolina's first theme park, visitors can board a train for a three-mile journey through the mountains and enjoy amusement rides and live entertainment throughout the park.

ANNUAL EVENTS

Black American Arts Festival, Greensboro—*January*

Edge of the World Snowboard Series, Boone—*January*

Annual Star Fiddlers Convention, Biscoe—*February*

Horse Trials, Tryon—*March*

Pig Cookin' Contest, Newport—*April*

Hang Gliding Spectacular, Nags Head—*May*

Hillsborough Hog Day—*June*

The Lost Colony Outdoor Drama, Manteo—*June*

Children's Day Fishing Tournament, Durham—*June*

Sand Sculpture Contest, Ocracoke—*July*

Highland Games and Gathering of Scottish Clans, Grandfather Mountain—*July–August*

North Carolina Apple Festival, Hendersonville—*September*

North Carolina Oyster Festival, Shallotte—*October*

National 500 Auto Race, Concord—*October*

State Fair, Raleigh—*October*

LEARN MORE ABOUT NORTH CAROLINA

BOOKS

General

Ayelsworth, Thomas. *The Lower Atlantic: North Carolina and South Carolina.* Broomall, PA: Chelsea House, 1995.

Highsmith, Carol M. *North Carolina: A Photographic Tour.* New York: Crescent Books, 1998.

Hintz, Martin, and Stephen Hintz. *North Carolina.* Danbury, CT: Children's Press, 1998. For older readers.

Special Interest

Lyons, Mary E. *Painting Dreams: Minnie Evans, Visionary Artist.* Boston, MA: Houghton Mifflin Company, 1996. North Carolinian Minnie Evans was a deeply religious woman who was haunted for years by dreams and decided to paint them. She is a celebrated African American folk artist.

Nichols, John. *Tobacco Road: The North Carolina Tar Heels Story (College Basketball Today).* Minnetonka, MN: Creative Education, 1999. This book follows the engaging story of the University of North Carolina at Chapel Hill basketball team.

Tillage, Leon Walter. *Leon's Story.* New York: Farrar, Straus & Giroux, 1997. This autobiography by the son of a sharecropper in Fuquay, North Carolina, gives a firsthand account of the years just before the civil rights movement began. Leon eventually joins the protests of Martin Luther King Jr.

Weatherford, Carole Boston. *Sink or Swim: African American Lifesavers of the Outer Banks.* Boston, MA: Houghton Mifflin Co., 1996. A collection of historical accounts of heroic African Americans who lived on the Outer Banks of North Carolina.

Fiction

Campbell, Donna. *Pale As the Moon.* Wilmington, NC: Coastal Carolina Press, 1999. This novel, set during the 1500s, tells of a friendship between a young Indian girl, Gray Squirrel, and a wild pony on one of North Carolina's Outer Banks islands. It examines the relationship between the Indians and the English settlers on Roanoke Island and offers an explanation for the missing colony.

Dowell, Frances O'Roark. *Dovey Coe.* New York: Atheneum, 2000. Spirited twelve-year-old Dovey is wrongly faced with a murder trial after her sister's suitor is mysteriously killed. A small town in the mountains of North Carolina is the setting for the trial.

Kline, Lisa Williams. *Eleanor Hill.* Asheville, NC: Front Street/ Cricket Books, 2000. Set in North Carolina in 1912, this novel tells the story of Eleanor Hill, who hopes to leave her small fishing village and see the world. Although her friends and family don't understand her desire for education and independence, she manages to follow her dreams.

WEBSITES

Official Web Site of North Carolina
<http://www.state.nc.us/>
The state government's web site offers helpful facts about North
Carolina's businesses, education, agencies, and other organizations.

Official North Carolina Travel Web Site
<http://www.visitnc.com/>
This site helps visitors to North Carolina choose interesting
destinations, activities, and events.

North Carolina Encyclopedia
<http://statelibrary.dcr.state.nc.us/nc/cover.html>
This online encyclopedia is designed to provide an overview of the
people, government, history, and resources of North Carolina.

North Carolina Secretary of State/ Kids' Page
<http://www.secretary.state.nc.us/kidspg/homepage.asp>
Visit this website for games, legends and ghost stories, and fun
facts, along with other interactive activities for young people.

The Raleigh News Observer
<http://www.news-observer.com>
Read about current events in North Carolina in the state capital's
newspaper.

PRONUNCIATION GUIDE

Albemarle (AL-buh-mahrl)

Catawba (kuh-TAW-buh)

Hatteras (HAT-ur-uhs)

Neuse (NOOS)

Piedmont (PEED-mahnt)

Raleigh (RAH-lee)

Roanoke (ROH-uh-nohk)

Soto, Hernando de (SOH-toh, her-NAHN-doh deh)

Tuscarora (tuhs-kuh-ROHR-uh)

Verrazano, Giovanni da (vehr-raht-SAHN-oh, joh-VAHN-nee dah)

The lighthouse at
Cape Hatteras

GLOSSARY

civil rights movement: a movement to gain equal rights, or freedoms, for all citizens—regardless of race, religion, or sex

colony: a territory ruled by a country some distance away

Fall Line: a line that follows the points at which high, rocky land drops to low, sandy soil. Numerous waterfalls are created along this line when rivers tumble from the upland to the lowland.

immigrant: a person who moves to a foreign country and settles there

Jim Crow laws: measures that separate black people from white people in public places, such as schools, parks, theaters, and restaurants. Jim Crow laws were enforced in the southern United States from 1877 to the 1950s.

nutrient: a material that serves to nourish, or feed, a living plant or animal

Outer Banks: long, narrow strips of sandy land off North Carolina's coast, separated from the mainland by a body of water

plantation: a large estate, usually in a warm climate, on which crops are grown by workers who live on the estate

precipitation: rain, snow, sleet, and hail

Reconstruction: the period from 1865 to 1877 during which the U.S. government brought the Southern states back into the Union after the Civil War

sound: a long inlet of water next to a coast, generally separating the mainland from an island or group of islands

wetland: a swamp, marsh, or other low, wet area that often borders a river, lake, or ocean

INDEX

PHOTO ACKNOWLEDGMENTS

Digital Cartographics, pp. 1, 8, 9, 50; © Franz-Marc Frei/Corbis, pp. 2–3; © Richard T. Nowitz/Corbis, p.3; © John R. Patton, pp 4 (detail), 17 (detail), 40 (detail), 52 (detail), 71 (bottom); © Danny Dempster, pp. 6, 73; © Jerry Hennen, pp. 7, 10, 25, 44, 45 (right); © Brent Parrett/New England Stock Photo, p. 11; © Frederica Georgia, pp. 12, 41, 46, 49; © Steve Warble/Mountain Magic, p. 13; © Mary A. Root/Root Resources, p. 14; © James P. Rowan, pp. 15, 16 (top); North Carolina Department of Travel and Tourism, pp. 16 (bottom), 45 (left), 80; North Carolina Department of Cultural Resources, Division of Archives and History, Historic Sites Section, pp. 17, 18, 20, 43; North Carolina Division of Archives and History, pp. 21, 24, 26, 29, 31, 32, 35, 36, 66 (second from top), 69 (bottom); Library of Congress, pp. 22, 34, 61, 69 (second from bottom); Bettmann/Corbis, p. 23; North Carolina Collection, University of North Carolina Library at Chapel Hill, pp. 28, 66 (top); The Charlotte Observer, p. 37; News & Record, Greensboro, NC/John "Jack" Moebes, p. 38; © Charles Gupton/Picturesque, p. 47; Chip Henderson/Picturesque, p. 48; Dave County Tourist Bureau, p. 51; © Jennifer Larson, p. 53; © W.A. Banaszewski/Visuals Unlimited, p. 54; © John D. Cunningham/Visuals Unlimited, p. 55; © William J. Weber/Visuals Unlimited, p. 56; Iredell Soil and Water Conservation District and USDA, Soil Conservation Service, Statesville, N.C., pp. 57 (top), 58, 59; © Gerry Lemmo, p. 57 (bottom); Tim Seeley, pp. 63, 71 (top), 72; Atlantic Records, p. 66 (second from bottom); Milton Blumenfeld, p. 66 (bottom); Hollywood Book and Poster, p. 67 (top, second from top, and second from bottom); Sara Lee Corp., p. 67 (bottom); National Education Association, p. 68 (top); Harlem Globetrotters, p. 68 (second from top); AP Photo/Wide World Photos, p. 68 (second from bottom); Independent Picture Service, p. 68 (bottom); © Michelle Broussard, p. 69 (top); Daytona International Speedway, p. 69 (second from top).

Front Cover: © Morton Beebe, S.F./Corbis (left), © Darrell Gulin/Corbis (right).